THE UNITED STATES OF EUROPE

MANIFESTO FOR A NEW EUROPE

Guy Verhofstadt

This book is published by the Federal Trust whose aim is to enlighten public debate on issues arising from the interaction of national, European and global levels of government. It does this in the light of its statutes which state that it shall promote 'studies in the principles of international relations, international justice and supranational government.'

Up-to-date information about the Federal Trust can be found on the internet at http://www.fedtrust.co.uk

© Guy Verhofstadt and Federal Trust
for Education and Research 2006

ISBN 1 903403 86 3

The Federal Trust is a Registered Charity No. 272241
7 Graphite Square, Vauxhall Walk,
London SE11 5EE

Company Limited by Guarantee No. 1269848

Printed in the European Union

TABLE OF CONTENTS

« *Un jour viendra où il n'y aura plus d'autres champs de bataille que les marchés s'ouvrant au commerce et les esprits s'ouvrant aux idées (...) Un jour viendra où l'on verra ces deux groupes immenses, les Etats-Unis d'Amérique, les Etats-Unis d'Europe placés en face l'un de l'autre, se tendant la main par-dessus les mers* »

Victor Hugo

« *(...) we must re-create the European Family in a regional structure called, it may be, the United States of Europe. If at first all the States of Europe are not willing or able to join the Union, we must nevertheless proceed to assemble and combine those who will and those who can. The salvation of the common people of every race and of every land from war or servitude must be established on solid foundations and must be guarded by the readiness of all men and women to die rather than submit to tyranny. Therefore I say to you: let Europe arise!* "

Winston Churchill

"*Nos pays sont devenus trop petits pour le monde actuel, à l'échelle des moyens techniques modernes, à la mesure de l'Amérique et de la Russie aujourd'hui, de la Chine et de l'Inde demain. L'unité des peuples européens réunis dans les Etats-Unis d'Europe est le moyen de relever leur niveau de vie et de maintenir la paix. Elle est le grand espoir et la chance de notre époque. Nous aussi, nous allons vers notre but, les Etats-Unis d'Europe, dans une course sans retour.*"

Jean Monnet

INTRODUCTION
TO PRIME MINISTER VERHOFSTADT'S BOOK

By Stefan Collignon
*Professor of European Political Economy, Harvard University
and London School of Economics*

The Prime Minister of Belgium, Guy Verhofstadt, has written a courageous and visionary book. It comes at the right time – in a period of flux when the future of Europe can be shaped. It adds to the reflection at a time when Verhofstadt's colleagues in the European Council have to find creative ways for overcoming Europe's confusion caused by the rejection of the Constitutional Treaty through French and Dutch referenda. The book offers new perspectives for Europe. It also reminds us of what we can learn from the creation of the American republic. It has an outstanding place in the long history of European intellectuals calling for the United States of Europe. Any reader who is concerned about the future of the European Union must read the Prime Minister's book.

"Like a house on fire" – this is how George Washington described the state of the American Confederation in 1787. A Union without proper government and lacking financial resources, a debt-burdened economy, rising social unrest and tensions between member states – all this seemed to confirm what sceptics in London had always predicted: that Americans were unfit to have their own government. Several months later, the Convention had met in Philadelphia and produced the Constitution of the United States of America. Rapidly ratified by 9 out of 13 member states, it has governed the United States to this day. George Washington had helped to extinguish the fire and became America's first President.

Today, the European house is on fire. Half a century after Europe's founding fathers set up the gradual process of European unification, the European dream seems to be fading. Like the early American Confederation, the European Union is run by "governance without government". Member states bicker about everything from financial resources to economic reforms. Politicians blame "Europe" for any unpopular decision and then regret that voters reject their projects. Despite the historic achievement of the single European market and the euro, unemployment has become a quasi-permanent style of life for millions of European citizens. Not surprisingly, citizens are disenchanted. Young men and women doubt that they still have a future in Europe and the brain drain across the Atlantic deprives Europe of its best minds.

European integration used to inspire people. It promised a better world. Not built on blood and tears, as earlier revolutions, it seemed to guarantee peace, democracy and prosperity. Its success has tempted many nations to join the Union. Yet, at the moment of its greatest triumph, when enlargement started to heal the wounds of a divided continent, the European Union seems to have lost the capacity to govern itself. The Belgian Prime Minster, Guy Verhofstadt, was the first to organise the fire brigade. Under his Presidency the European Council in Laeken set up the European Convention responsible for writing a Constitutional Treaty for the European Union. But contrary to the American example, ratification has failed. Since then, the speechless European heads of state and government have agreed on "a period for reflection". But again Guy Verhofstadt is refusing to watch how the European house is burning to the ground. This book is his call for action.

What went wrong with the European Union? What needs to be done? As a seasoned statesman, Guy Verhofstadt gives us the answer: Europe is not capable of acting decisively when facing the challenges of a globalised economy and the socio-economic consequences of demographic changes. The problem is the intergovernmental form of governance. For many citizens, Europe is synonymous with a Kafkaesque maze of bureaucracy that meddles with the insignificant but does not solve the essential.

Political economists can help to explain why this Europe is failing. They observe a growing number of policy areas where public goods are provided that affect all citizens across the Union. This is most apparent in the economic domain, where single market regulations are necessary for protecting consumers and creating a level playing field for producers. For citizens in Euroland, who use the same currency, these common public goods are even more important. The rate of inflation determines the value of their savings; the interest rate sets the conditions for their financing a mortgage or buying a car; the exchange rate determines external price competitiveness. All this has consequences for jobs, economic growth and standards of living – regardless of whether one lives in Brussels, Helsinki, the Algarve or Crete.

But not all public goods are the same. Some can easily be provided by voluntary cooperation between autonomous governments, because every member state has an interest in participating in their production. They are called *inclusive* public goods. Famous examples are Airbus, the Galileo satellite system and some domains of technological research and development. However, there exists also a large and growing domain, where this logic does not apply. The related *exclusive* public goods are characterised by the fact that individual countries may be temped to free-ride on the efforts made by others.

For example, the Stability and Growth Pact covers such exclusive public goods. If all member states apply the rules of the Pact strictly, interest rates will be low. But then it will be advantageous for every government to borrow cheaply rather than raise taxes for additional expenditure. As a consequence, every member state has an incentive to do the opposite of what would be beneficial for all. For this reason, different policy regimes are necessary to provide these different forms of public goods efficiently. Inclusive public goods can be provided by intergovernmental policy cooperation; exclusive public goods require a single government to ensure that no member state can free-ride at the expense of all others.

Verhofstadt refers to the long and fruitless debate in Europe between those who favour the "community method" of delegating competences to the European level and inter-governmentalists, who prefer a Europe of independent nations. This debate has always missed the essential point: each policy regime is appropriate for a specific class of public goods. Much confusion in policy debates is due to the fact that people mix up the two different policy domains.

But Prime Minister Verhofstadt provides a clear solution to the problem. Just like in any parliamentary democracy, Europe needs a genuine European government with executive powers to deal with policy areas dominated by exclusive European public goods. This government must have its own resources, financed by a European tax. It should be led by a President, who will emerge from direct democratic elections for the European Parliament. It does not matter whether one calls such a regime the *United States of Europe* or a *European Republic*, as others have suggested. The point is that only a proper European government can ensure the provision of exclusive public goods. In an ever-closer Union this is the only way for citizens to be governed efficiently. But it is also impossible to delegate more policy areas to Europe, unless citizens have a right to vote and select the policy package they prefer. In a democracy, efficiency and legitimacy reinforce each other.

The notion of the United States of Europe has a long history. Jean-Jacques Rousseau saw a Europe, where "there are no more French, German, Spanish, even Englishmen whatever one says, there are only Europeans. They all have the same tastes, the same passions the same habits". Montesquieu noted, "Matters are such in Europe that all states need each other. Europe's a state made up of several provinces". Kant proposed the creation of a confederation of European states as a step toward a "world republic". Victor Hugo saw the day coming "when you France, you Russia, you England, you Germany, when all you Nations of the continent, without losing distinctive qualities or your individual glories, will bind yourself tightly together into a single entity and you will come to constitute a European fraternity, as absolutely as Brittany, Burgundy and Alsace are now bound together with France". He also emphasised that "the European Federal Republic is established in right and is waiting to be established in fact."

After the disaster of World War I, the German Social Democratic Party put the creation of the United Stated of Europe into its 1926 party programme in Heidelberg and it reiterated this commitment again after 1945. In 1930, the United States of Europe became the title of a book by Edouard Herriot – Prime Minister in France's Third Republic – and constituted a serious attempt at practically envisioning a unified Europe. Within the framework of the erstwhile League of Nations, it promoted the idea of a coalition of all willing European states to foster the organisation of economic and security policies in Europe. The notion of a "United States of Europe" received most attention in the well-known speech by Winston Churchill in Zurich (1946) where he called upon Europe to "arise!". Jean Monnet founded the Action Committee for the United States of Europe in 1955 after the French Assemblée Nationale had rejected the Treaty on the European Defence Community.

More than two centuries after Rousseau, the United States of Europe is still not yet a reality. Should one conclude that the idea is utopian and impossible? Or does it not simply mean that the time has not been ripe yet? Half a century after the Treaty of Rome, the world has changed. It is also time for Europe's institutions to change. Jean Monnet was perfectly aware that "one change begets another" and "men are changed by what they do." He frequently used the image from his Alpine walking tours, whereby the perspective shifted minimally but inexorably all the time as one climbed the mountain. And the chalet at the top would not be the same as in the valley.

Today the process of economic and political integration has reached a point where Europe has to adapt its governance to a political Union with full democracy. Otherwise it will perish. Who could seriously believe that in a world of 6 bn people, growing to 9 bn by 2050, Europe's mini-states, where even the largest will represent less than one percent of the world population, could still attempt to shape their destiny?

In Prime Minster Verhofstadt's vision, the United States of Europe is not the dreaded super-state, a Leviathan that asphyxiates all personal initiative. In fact, his proposal is totally coherent with modern political economy. He selects seven policy areas, which are dominated by exclusive public goods. This *res publica* will be administered by the European government. Nothing more, nothing less. Peoples' identity – their identification with culture, traditions, customs – are not affected by their right to choose the direction and the leaders of their common government. I find it reassuring that this United States of Europe is built on citizens' interests rather than on peoples' feelings.

The question remains: how shall Europe get to Verhofstadt's Promised Land? Clearly the project of the United States of Europe is more ambitious than the failed Constitutional Treaty, of which Verhofstadt says that it was a "watered down version" of the Convention draft, which did not go down well with citizens. Maybe no compromise is better than a bad compromise. It seems obvious, however, that a new Constitution needs to be written. Of course, the Belgian Prime Minister needs to be discreet on the subject of what to do next. He will negotiate with his colleagues in the European Council. But he does insist that the United States of Europe needs to be approved by a European-wide referendum. Given that he also mentions favourably the ratification procedure in the USA, where a quorum of states (9/13) was required to approve the Constitution, it may not be far-fetched to imagine the modalities of a new European-wide referendum.

However, we all know that the EU is not a politically homogenous bloc. Some countries have a long tradition of sitting on the fence, even if they wish to benefit from the large and unified European market. Others have only recently gained their national freedom and autonomy and they may not wish to trade this in for the benefits of European public goods. With remarkable clarity, Prime Minister Verhofstadt explains how he intends to cut the Gordian knot of dealing with Eurosceptics. Countries belonging to the Eurozone share more exclusive public goods than those who have retained their own currency. They therefore face different problems of governance. Hence, it is logically coherent to think that Euroland will form the nucleus of the United States of Europe. By endowing themselves with an efficient government capable of meeting the economic and political challenges of the future, these countries will also protect the interest of those who do not wish to make the full step to the United States of Europe. The single market could not survive without the euro. The new Organisation of European States, proposed by the Prime Minister, will then become the framework, where the United States of Europe cooperates with its European partners. One may describe this by the image of "building the house of political Union in the garden of economic Union". Verhofstadt has clear concepts for both the house and the garden. Note, however, how open and flexible his proposed structure is: any country joining European monetary union is qualified to become a member state of the United States of Europe. This is a welcome alternative to two-speed models of integration, where a *directoire* of large member states takes over power, thereby depriving citizens of their democratic right to choose jointly their preferred policies.

Guy Verhofstadt's book is a true act of courage. It is written at a time when political cynicism dominates public discourse. Politicians are mostly portrayed as power-hungry, self-serving rational utility maximisers. All too often the sacrifices are forgotten that public service imposes on those who choose that career. A frequently voiced complaint is that Europe is in a sad state, because we miss men and women of vision and conviction, like de Gaulle and Adenauer, Schmidt and Giscard, Kohl and Mitterrand and Delors. Have we forgotten how vilified these men were in their own time? In any case, the charge would be misdirected at Prime Minister Verhofstadt. He has demonstrated, again and again, his conviction, courage and genuine love for Europe, as well as for his country. In this book, Prime Minister Verhofstadt defends the project of the United States of Europe – the only project so far capable of linking coherently the European dream with practical means. Like all new things, it is an intriguing and somewhat disquieting idea. Who does not know the comfort of following the established opinion? Who has not experienced the discomfort of thought, which obliges us to find new, untrodden paths? The American statesman and 7th President, Andrew Jackson, is known for the sentence: "One man with courage makes a majority". We all can be men and women of courage who will make the United States of Europe.

PROLOGUE

Fifteen years ago, a page of history was turned. The implosion of the Soviet Union brought a bipolar world tumbling down, leaving in its wake a disjointed patchwork of new countries, and the United States as the world's sole, undisputed political and military superpower.

However, new economic rivals are emerging in the East, where major centres of development like China and India are undergoing unprecedented transformation, following the trail blazed by Japan. Indeed, within just a few years, Asia has single-handedly shifted the focus of the world economy, a development that looks certain to gain further impetus in the future. After all, in some parts of Southeast Asia, the economy is growing 10 times as fast as it is in Europe, and many people feel concerned that these new economic heavyweights are suddenly helping to determine the prices of the clothes we buy and the cost of our petrol.

Economic growth in China, India and Japan, which between them are home to two-and-a-half billion people, will also translate into greater political influence. That is the natural run of things, and it is already clear that in a few years' time the world will have four major powers: the United States, China, India and Japan.

What role will Europe still be playing? European unification was once a most promising project. But today the European Union is politically divided and economically weakened. On key occasions, like the war in Iraq, the Union has failed to speak with one voice. Economically too, we appear to have lost momentum. Our prosperity is under pressure from increasing globalisation, a challenge to which the Union is responding, once again, in a non-unified, ponderous manner. So it's hardly surprising that more and more of our citizens are entertaining doubts about Europe.

If Europe intends to be a true world player in the future, it must become more closely integrated. Only a 'United States of Europe' that is capable of acting decisively can rise to the challenges facing us and meet citizens' expectations. So we must let the Union switch direction. Europe must stop being patronising and should leave the Member States in peace to deal with issues that they are better equipped to tackle. At the same time Europe will have to concentrate on a few major tasks.

The first task of the 'United States of Europe' is to develop a joint strategy for rising to the two main socio-economic challenges currently facing Europe, namely globalisation and our ageing population. Globalisation exerts pressure on the European social model from outside the Union, whilst the ageing of its population exerts pressure from within. Providing a well-targeted response to both trends is the best way of combating weak economic growth and high unemployment. The basis of this joint strategy is convergence, determining minimum and maximum requirements, including in areas such as social protection and taxation, to serve as the basis for the Member States' future development. In this way the European economy can become competitive again without descending to social dumping. The 'United States of Europe' will also have to step up its efforts in the areas of research and development and the establishment of trans-European information networks. Furthermore, we will need a single European area of justice and security if we are to fight crime more effectively. Finally, we need to set up joint armed forces and conduct a foreign policy through which Europe speaks with one voice.

Only if Europe adopts a unified approach in all these areas will Europe really count as a world player. Preferably, all the Union's Member States should take part, but if this proves impossible, all the countries belonging to the euro zone plus those set to join it shortly should be mobilised. In such a scenario, Europe will comprise two concentric circles: a political core, a 'United States of Europe' based on the euro zone, and surrounding it a confederation of countries, or 'Organisation of European States'.

Naturally, the political core must never oppose any form of broader cooperation. All those Member States that wish to join it, old or new, should be able to do so. The sole precondition should be their willingness to work unconditionally on pushing ahead with the overall political project.

The notion of a 'United States of Europe' is the only option for the old continent. After all, it makes no sense for us all to retain holds over each other and continue bickering about which path to go down, whilst other continents sail merrily past us. We face a clear choice: We can either do nothing and remain sidelined, or we can embrace reform and become an active world player. I suggest we opt for a 'United States of Europe'.

EUROPE IN CRISIS

Europe is in crisis, not merely weathering a passing storm, but facing serious questions about the European project per se. For generations, the unification of Europe was held up as a major ideal, marking an end to the constant wars on the Old Continent, clashes that were really European civil wars. Moreover, on the ruins left by two World Wars Europe created durable democracy, burgeoning prosperity and a decent level of social protection.

When France, Germany, Italy, The Netherlands, Belgium and Luxembourg signed the Treaty of Rome in 1957, they had a specific objective in mind: to develop a close-knit community and form a Union capable of guaranteeing peace and ensuring prosperity.

Right from the outset, the project of European unification proved highly attractive. Peoples from all corners or Europe wanted to be part of the Union, especially those enduring a military dictatorship, like the Greeks, Spaniards or Portuguese. It was partly down to the European Union that they found the strength to embark on the path leading towards democracy and cast off the yoke of dictatorship once and for all.

After the fall of the Berlin Wall and the collapse of the Soviet Union, the dream of a united Europe really lay within reach. Back in 1989, nobody doubted that the lost sons and daughters in Eastern European had to rejoin the European family as soon as possible. That happened just 15 years later, on 1 May 2004, when eight former Eastern bloc countries plus Cyprus and Malta joined the European Union. So membership remains an attractive proposition, and even now a number of countries are knocking on the door of the European Union.

Then one year later, in spring 2005, the Constitutional Treaty that was intended to give the enlarged Europe fresh foundations was rejected in referenda held in both France and the Netherlands. This prompted other countries to postpone their ratification of the European Constitution indefinitely, i.e. basically to shelve it. The major fear now is that the European Constitution is dead in the water. And insult was added to injury in July 2005 when the European Council failed to reach agreement on the future financing of the Union.

All of a sudden, enthusiasm for the European project appears to have ebbed away completely, making room for indifference and fear. Fear of 'hordes from the East' coming over here to snatch work away from the local populace. Fear of seeing our own companies move their operations to one of the new EU Member States. Fear of competition from the economies in Southeast Asia or of Chinese textiles that will spell doom for their European rivals. And fear, too, of organised crime running amok, unbridled in the enlarged Europe.

Analysis of the referenda results in France and the Netherlands indicate that the European project can still rely on full support from older people in particular. These are individuals who have lived through a war and understand that European unification put an end to hostilities, a fact that is incidentally unique in world history. Never before have so many countries voluntarily relinquished some of their sovereignty for the sake of peace and prosperity. And never before has international cooperation proved so successful.

By contrast, younger people are less convinced. For them the horrors of the Great War and World War II are pictures in history books. For them, European unification is no longer an ideal, but a simple fact. They travel through Europe. They study at the many European universities and colleges. They speak several languages. For them, the existence of Europe is so obvious, they don't stop to think about it. And if they do, then they think of 'Brussels', which is synonymous with the reaching of incomprehensible compromises, a Mount Olympus that interferes with absolutely everything, like Kafka's castle, a maze of bureaucracy that costs loads of money. In a nutshell, Europe does not inspire the younger generations.

Admittedly, inspiration depends on choices, choices that Europe has signally failed to provide. After all, we live in a single market without customs posts or borders. We have a single currency, the euro. Bit by bit Europe has accomplished various, mainly economic, objectives without really matching them with political counterparts. The choice of the political direction that Europe ought to take has never been publicly revealed.

Having said that, various attempts have been made to provide direction, the latest occurring five years ago in the French coastal town of Nice where European leaders adopted a declaration in which they all undertook to map out a new path for the European Union, a path that was more in line with the desires of Europe's citizens and mindful of their grumbles. The following year, in Laeken here in Belgium, the debate on this new direction finally got under way. A European Convention was set up, comprising representatives of the respective national governments and parliaments and of the European institutions. The fruit of the Convention's activities was a draft Constitution that would assign the Union new tasks and give it new instruments, enabling it to play a leading role in a world that is becoming more and more global with every day that passes. Ultimately, as is so often the case, European leaders adopted a watered-down version of the draft Constitution which did not go down at all well with citizens, at least not in the Netherlands and France.

Admittedly, far from unearthing a new crisis, the French and Dutch referenda revealed a latent sense of discomfort beneath the surface that has been widespread in Europe for some time now. So we have to grasp the nettle and ask ourselves how things could reach this stage. What is the answer? Where should we go from here? Clearly, Europe is at a crossroads, faced with what actually comes down to a pretty simple choice: either we allow Europe to atrophy into a mere free trade area in which the Member States compete with each other to see who can come up with the best response to globalisation, or we take up the European thread once more and create a close-knit political Europe that is capable of playing a role at global level and fashions for itself the instruments required to modernise the European economy and thereby respond to the very phenomena which breathe fear into the continent's citizens today.

It all boils down to making the European project attractive again for younger generations of Europeans and also finding a way of responding to people's everyday concerns. It is precisely these issues that this manifesto sets out to address.

CONFLICTING SIGNALS

Since 1992, a thorough opinion poll has been conducted amongst the population of Europe twice a year. This 'Eurobarometer' asks citizens of the European Union about all kinds of issues, such as their confidence in the European institutions, or about Europe's relations with the United States. It also sounds out the direction they believe Europe should take in the longer run.

One conspicuous result of the latest Eurobarometer survey (conducted in summer 2005, i.e. after the referenda) is the extensive agreement among Europe's population about the direction in which Europe ought to move. People don't want less Europe, they want more Europe. Thus, three out of four Europeans want to see a common defence policy. Two-thirds of Europeans want there to be a Common Foreign Policy. Many European citizens also hold the view that the European project needs to make faster progress in a number of areas. Only in seven of the 25 Member States do citizens feel that Europe has already done enough integrating. What is more, 50% of citizens believe that within the next few years Europe will come to play a more prominent role in their daily lives. Just one in seven regrets this and believes that Europe should play a lesser role. A large majority of Europeans also want Europe to develop into a political union, and a similarly clear proportion is in favour of the euro being introduced in all European countries. Only Denmark, Greece, Sweden, Malta and the United Kingdom have no majority in favour of this.

The Eurobarometer also shows that European unification gives rise to uncertainties. For instance, 75% of Europeans believe that jobs will shift to other EU Member States, to countries with lower production costs. Nearly two-thirds of Europeans fear an increase in drug trading and a rise in organised crime. The same proportion maintain that their respective country is paying a continuously mounting contribution to the European Union.

Three consecutive Eurobarometers (June 2003, January 2004 and November 2004) asked no fewer than 25,000 citizens from the 25 Member States about the future European Constitution. A clear majority deemed a Constitution necessary, felt that there should be an EU foreign minister, that a European President ought to be appointed, and that the European Parliament needed to be given greater powers.

In fact, if these results are anything to go by, there can be little discussion about the direction in which European citizens want the Union to head. They want to see more European integration and to see a Europe that takes greater responsibility. One thing they definitely do not want is less Europe. Notwithstanding that, the referenda went amiss. Why? What were the causes of this breakdown? Is the Eurobarometer inaccurate? Naturally, any opinion poll has a certain margin of error, but the majorities emerging from the Eurobarometer surveys are so overwhelming and have been constant for so many years now that it makes more sense to seek an explanation elsewhere.

WHY DID SO MANY CITIZENS VOTE 'NO'?

François Mitterrand once said that referenda never elicit an answer to the question put in them. Consequently, many politicians and political commentators oppose the holding of referenda, especially where the European Constitution is concerned. They contend that subject matter like the Constitution is too difficult for the public, which cannot even read it, let alone understand it. Instead, it is argued, when citizens make their choice, they allow themselves to be led by their degree of satisfaction or discontentment at that particular moment. Even the weather on the day of the referendum can swing the outcome of the vote, it is claimed.

However, it would be too easy to attribute the 'no' vote to these causes. It is fair to say that no referendum is ever solely about the question it is designed to ask, just as it is correct to say that the more difficult the compromise being voted on, the lower the chance of a positive result. But is that not what democracy is all about? If the popular view is that the Constitution provides no response to people's grumbles, or fails to meet their expectations, then clearly there is a problem. If politicians cannot convince them that the draft text they produced answers their doubts and concerns, then it is legitimate to speak of a schism. Often, it is only when citizens are given the chance to speak out in a referendum that their doubts and concerns surface. This is how referenda can elicit unexpected results and force the duly 'ambushed' politicians to change tack. And that is what the referenda conducted over the last few months have done too. The resounding 'no' in the Netherlands and France is compelling us to review the European Community's achievements in a bid to come up with new recipes and concepts derived from them.

The first thing we need is an accurate assessment of the situation. Dozens of analyses have been performed in recent months. Many of them list national, domestic reasons as key factors. Many citizens evidently used their referendum on the European Constitution as a vehicle to express dissatisfaction with their respective country's national policy. And even though just a small minority of the population turned against the Constitution for that reason, this indubitably helped to make a difference in the result. However, it goes without saying that Europe has little sway over this factor.

Accordingly, we must focus on the other causes of the 'no' vote, and they can be roughly summed up as falling under two dominant feelings: fear and doubt. Fears of a number of worldwide developments, like globalisation and delocalisation, that are racing towards us at breakneck speed, and at the same time doubts about whether Europe is capable of offering an adequate response.

Let us start off by considering fear. People fear for their jobs and are frightened about losing their level of prosperity. We are living in an era of economic upheavals. New electronic media like the Internet and e-mail have banished borders between countries and continents to the virtual domain. Globalisation has opened up new markets and brought us products amazingly fast. That is the positive aspect. However, the fear is that some new economies with their cheap manpower and substandard social security will not only outcompete our companies, condemning them to death, but also that our companies will delocalise. The relevant statistics suggest that these fears are not unfounded. Between 1992 and 2002 economic growth in the euro zone averaged not even 2%, whereas growth in the United States topped 3%. Over that same period, employment also rose by just 6.5% here in Europe, compared with 17% in the USA. The gap with China is far greater still, and looks certain to grow even larger in the near future. In short, people have the feeling that globalisation is changing the face of the planet extremely fast, and sense that a battle with winners and losers is unfolding. And what Europe's citizens fear is that we will gradually end up amongst the losers and become the first victims.

This main fear is compounded by another, namely the fear of society disintegrating or at least the feeling that we can no longer sustain our present solid social system. People hold the ageing of our society to blame for this, but also point the finger at Europe itself. People have the impression that all that Europe is concerned about is opening up markets and that it hardly pays any attention to safeguarding the European Social Model. Consequently, they fear they may only barely receive their pension, if they receive one at all, and that unemployment benefit will drop so far as to push people into poverty. They fear that medical care will become unaffordable or that they may end up on long waiting lists for treatment.

In recent years, this twofold fear about people losing both their jobs and a decent social safety net has been greatly amplified by the enlargement of the European Union. After the collapse of the Soviet Union, every European citizen strongly favoured action that would undo the division of their continent once and for all and scoop up all the Eastern European countries and peoples in a United Europe. However, that spirit of hospitality very soon turned to fear about being overwhelmed by 'Polish plumbers or construction workers'. Furthermore, people fear that if Europe intends to remain competitive, it will have to scale back its social standards instead of raising those in Eastern Europe. In itself, this fear is nothing new, having surfaced during previous phases of enlargement too. For when Greece, Spain and Portugal joined the ranks of Europe's Member States, some people predicted 'a flood of cheap labour that would engulf the old Member States'. Yet not only did such a flood never materialise, the countries in question were not broadly perceived by the public as foreign or threatening. After all, they had become popular holiday destinations, where many pensioners intended to go and settle. The accession to the EU of the Scandinavian countries and the United Kingdom failed to prompt any fear either, for these were countries with a similar level of prosperity. Where the 10 new Member States are concerned, the situation is clearly different. For not only are they far less prosperous, we barely know them, if at all.

But on top of this fear of job loss and the erosion of social protection, primed by the enlargement of the Union, large swathes of citizens also fear losing their own identity. This rather vague feeling is undoubtedly a result of globalisation and a number of unfortunate decisions taken by the European institutions which, through excessive regulatory zeal, impinged on deeply anchored traditions and customs which people hold extremely dear and which give them something solid to hold onto in life. Take the directives stipulating how French cheese has to be made. So some directives or proposals have elicited great indignation from large sectors of the population and needlessly exacerbated a sense of loss of identity.

Finally, there is also the fear of the spread of organised crime. Over the past decade, people have seen for themselves how the place where they live has been made unsafe by marauding gangs, often of Eastern European origin. Good work by the police and closer cooperation between police forces in various neighbouring countries mean that more and more of these criminal gangs are being rounded up. But the impression remains that these gangs only started appearing after the EU's internal borders were abolished. On top of this, various terrorist attacks perpetrated both inside and outside Europe, and murders like that of Theo Van Gogh, have merely deepened people's feeling of insecurity and their fear of foreigners.

All these fearful imaginings, and probably most of all the fear of loss of identity, were bolstered even further by the recent decision by the European Council to launch accession negotiations with Turkey. European citizens have not yet had a chance to digest thoroughly the membership of the former Communist countries, yet they already find themselves faced with the decision to recognise Turkey as a candidate Member State. And while the broad consensus regarding the former Eastern bloc is that the countries in question genuinely belong to the European family, with Turkey there is far from such agreement. And even though I back both the decision itself and its timing, we ought to be honest and admit that the ratification of the new Constitution and Turkey's approval as a candidate Member State have proved too much for our citizens to swallow all at once.

All these feelings of trepidation call for an efficacious policy, though citizens have their doubts as to whether the European Union is capable of delivering in this respect. At the very least, a majority of French and Dutch voters decided that the Constitution, at least in its current form, did not constitute the right response to the questions, doubts and uncertainties pervading the minds of the public. Many citizens who voted 'no' in the referenda did so because in their view Europe lacks the right powers and instruments to conduct a genuinely effective policy. Why transfer even more funds from national treasuries to the European Union if no efficient policy results? The contribution to the European Union totals barely one fortieth of the resources available to the governments of the national Member States. Nonetheless, people deem this modest payment to be excessive if the ensuing results prove unsatisfactory.

In other words, even though Europe's citizens also favour continued European integration, what they want above all is a strong Europe that works smoothly and efficiently, a Europe that offers a response to the concerns that have arisen over the last few years. Yet they retain serious doubts about the latter in particular. Why cede ever more powers and resources to a Union that may be expanding every day, but otherwise seems incapable of offering an answer to the most pressing challenges?

In short, the Union's citizens want Europe to be stronger, more purposeful and, well, *different*. They do not want a Europe that merely churns out paper or opens up its borders. They are not willing to pay for that alone. What they *do* want is a decisive Europe that develops a foreign policy and a credible security and defence policy and above all comes up with a comprehensive economic and social strategy that is capable of rising to the challenges posed by globalisation. Put another way, Europe's citizens want a European project that is once again characterised by positive action and which inspires them. If Europe is to succeed in doing this, it must make a clearer choice, a choice that it has repeatedly postponed making in the past.

FROM THE HAGUE TO BRUSSELS

The dream of refashioning Europe into a political Union has remained largely that: just a dream, albeit one that was pursued right from the early stages of European unification. Both during and just after World War II the need for a United Europe was professed in the most emphatic terms. In 1946 Churchill called for "a kind of United States of Europe". In 1948, at the Hague Congress, a majority of the delegates called for a political Europe, but the project was torpedoed by a number of countries.

Three years later France, Germany, Italy, the Netherlands, Belgium and Luxembourg took a first step towards closer economic cooperation when they set up the European Coal and Steel Community (ECSC). Another three years later, in 1954, the same six founding countries joined forces to set up a European Defence Community and associated Political Union. Their proposal suggested a two-chamber system, one chamber comprising directly elected MPs, and the other being made up of existing MPs from the respective national parliaments. There would be a single foreign policy and a European army would be established, its ranks filled with members of the military from all the participating countries.

After the European Defence Community had been approved and ratified by the six countries in question, under the influence of Charles De Gaulle it was rejected by the French *Assemblée nationale*, whereupon Jean Monnet, the driving force behind European unification, set up an Action Committee for the United States of Europe, a movement designed to generate some fresh momentum. A little later on, prompted by this initiative and other factors, Paul-Henri Spaak convened his colleagues in Messina and Brussels with a view to taking a new and major step towards Europe's economic integration. In 1957 the six founding countries duly signed the Treaty of Rome, creating the European Economic Community (EEC). The EEC's main aim was to ensure the free movement of goods, people, services and capital.

Even after that date, various attempts were made to build the European Economic Community into a fully-fledged political entity: the Fouchet Plan in 1961, the Tindemans Report in 1975 and the Spinelli Report in 1984. All these plans were enthusiastically received, but once again there was always at least one country that did not accept them. However, this does not mean that no progress was made. For instance, in 1979 Members of the European Parliament were directly elected for the first time.

But the main headway was made in economic unification, thanks to Jacques Delors. In 1986, on the basis of his White Paper, the so-called Single European Act was adopted, finally making the free movement of goods, services, people and capital a reality in the European Community. That in turn led to the Maastricht Treaty in 1992, which triggered the establishment of the Economic and Monetary Union and the introduction of the euro.

Yet we may safely state that Maastricht also marked the start of a salvo of warning shots aimed at European leaders. The Danes voted against the Maastricht Treaty, whilst in France the referendum was only won by the 'yes'-voters by the narrowest of margins. In 2001 Ireland voted against the Treaty of Nice. Then in 2003, in another referendum the Swedes rejected the introduction of the euro in their country. In the end, a few deft adjustments were made for Denmark and Ireland, which duly played along in a second referendum.

In the 1990s, mounting opposition to European construction was fuelled quite substantially by the use of so-called opt-outs and opt-ins, granting exceptions from European treaties to Member States that had chosen to become members of the European Union but did not (or not yet) wish to participate in all areas of policy. Separately from this, the British received a rebate on their contribution to the European Community in 1984 after Margaret Thatcher famously said: "I want my money back". After the Maastricht Treaty, differences of opinion on the path to be followed were increasingly 'solved' by introducing such exceptions. For instance, not all the Member States are involved in Schengen. Not everyone opted to introduce the euro. And on the social front a number of countries were granted an opt-out, like the United Kingdom, which in 1989 decided not to sign the Social Charter (Charter of the Fundamental Social Rights of Workers). Bit by bit a multi-speed Union has taken shape, a type of 'à la carte Europe' in which not all Member States automatically subscribe to all areas of policy, which are sometimes even openly criticised by those onlookers remaining on the sidelines. However well-intentioned it may be at the outset, the use of permanent, invariably applicable exceptions is a highly questionable practice that does no favours whatsoever to the European Union's image, because such opt-outs show that it does not really matter whether or not all the Member States are marching in the same direction. In actual fact, opt-outs constitute a de facto negation of the idea of European cooperation.

Consequently, it should come as no surprise to us that no real breakthrough was made in spite of the Maastricht Treaty. The Treaty of Amsterdam did decide to embrace a European foreign policy, but the first High Representative for the Common Foreign and Security Policy, Javier Solana, has only limited room for manoeuvre. The Treaty of Nice adopted three years later did create a

European Security and Defence Policy, but this went no further than the cataloguing on paper of a number of military capabilities. And the few operations developed by the Union in recent years are still very much dragging their feet.

After a seemingly interminable row over votes and seats in the Council and Parliament, lasting four days and four nights, at that same summit in Nice, people became aware that we could not go on like this. Not for nothing was a Declaration on the Future of Europe adopted alongside the actual treaty itself, starting out from the idea that a clear choice had to be made. If the European Union failed to take another major step forwards, there was a danger that it would falter and descend into bickering and infighting. In any case there seemed no point in convening another co-called Intergovernmental Conference, because bringing together 25 heads of government and hoping for a breakthrough seems a barely feasible option.

That is why the European Council in Laeken, Belgium, decided to adopt a new, ground-breaking approach, embodied by the European Convention. Under the leadership of Valéry Giscard d'Estaing, a global draft Constitution for Europe was drawn up by a body comprising over 100 delegates, representing all the governments and parliaments of the 25 Member States, as well as the European Parliament and the European Commission. The Convention broke some long-established taboos, such as introducing the notion of a 'Constitutional Treaty', creating the post of European foreign minister or expanding decision-making based on qualified majority votes.

And yet it all failed to amount to much. Important choices made by the Convention were nullified again by the Intergovernmental Conference. The heads of government duly worked some more on refashioning the Constitution, modifying it in such a way that the beginnings of cohesion hidden behind the text were further diluted.

EUROPE: UNKNOWN AND UNLOVED

Nevertheless, the basis underlying the European Constitution remains fully intact. There remains a need to turn the European Union into a comprehensive, coherent political project capable of providing answers to the many fresh challenges we now find ourselves facing. Everyone feels that the European Union is not presently capable of doing this, a feeling that derives from a more general dissatisfaction with how things are going. Europe, which is usually patronisingly referred to as 'Brussels', is further removed than ever from the ideal cherished by mere mortals. To the man or woman in the street it is clear that instead of busying itself with essentials, like jobs or crime, Europe is futilely wasting its time dealing with issues in a manner that is anyway often felt to be annoying, such as stipulating the sizes of battery chicken cages or the ingredients of jam, as set out in the breakfast directive. And although the number of EU officials is no more than the number employed by an average European city, the Union nonetheless finds itself struggling against an incredibly technocratic – and above all bureaucratic – image and tarred with an awful reputation for wasting money.

The fact that Europe has such an unenviable reputation should come as no surprise. For years, Europe has been abused by national politicians, made the scapegoat whenever less than popular measures had to be adopted in a Member State. In addition, for a long time Europe was simply nothing new. The credit for any successes and positive achievements scored by the European Union was invariably hijacked at national level. And not a single politician opted to stand up for Europe when things were going slightly less well. Take the introduction of the euro, probably the biggest success story relating to European unification. Barely five years later citizens are still only seeing disadvantages, unjustly blaming Europe for the price rises that went hand in hand with the introduction of the euro. There *were* business people and traders in various Member States in the euro zone who cashed in on the fact that consumers were not familiar with the new currency by putting up their prices. There were also national politicians in the respective Member States who neglected to take action against them and who also failed to make the euro a driving force behind a common economic policy. All that remains today is a sour aftertaste, and in certain circles in some countries there is open speculation about abolishing the euro. So lack of ambition can make even the most successful instrument of integration come under fire.

Furthermore, over the past 20 years nobody has taken the trouble of properly explaining the ongoing changes in Europe. The European institutions have done too little in this respect, or not been successful enough in their endeavours. The same goes for national leaders, some of whom hold the view that Europe is a fig leaf that can be used to cover up their own domestic failures, knowing that they can merrily bash away at Europe, safe in the knowledge that it will never hit back. This explains how an image of inefficiency arose over time, an image of a Union that is 'bad', that does without any support from national politicians and is itself incapable of selling its own accomplishments to the public. European summits have degenerated into arenas where points have to be scored in the national interests of one's own country. Only now and then do we hear convincing speeches defending the general interests of Europe.

This trend reached its nadir (so far) at the European Council held in June 2005 where a decision was made not to take any decisions, leaving Member States free to opt whether or not to go ahead and ratify the European Constitution. Moreover, the participants failed to reach agreement about the financing of the Union. The only consensus reached was that the time had come – again! – to choose the direction in which the European Union should develop in future. It is not fanciful to think that the Union is beginning to unravel, like the Growth and Stability Pact, whereby a number of countries don't give a damn about the shared rules and once again allow themselves to be driven by national reflexes.

A FREE TRADE AREA OR A POLITICAL EUROPE?

Put bluntly, Europe can be constructed in line with two main models, the first being a 'Europe of Nations', as advocated by Charles De Gaulle, namely an intergovernmental model that primarily takes account of national interests, and the second being a federal Europe or Community-based approach, a Union of citizens, not just Member States, seeking to act in the general interest of the European Union as a whole. Ever since the European Union was established, it has been wrestling with these two approaches, and in actual fact there is a fundamental difference of opinions here that has never been cleared up, a clash between federalists on the one hand and so-called 'intergovernmentalists' on the other.

The same difference of opinion is evident in economic policy. The groups of countries advocating each opinion not only view economic policy or the European Social Model through different eyes, but also hold up a different vision of European integration. Some see the Union primarily as a free trade area, and others want to continue building Europe into a fully fledged political Union.

However, it would be wrong to regard these two groups as static entities. Countries sometimes shift from one camp to the other over a period of years. For instance, some countries pretty recently abandoned the federalist group and went over to the intergovernmentalists. In addition, some of the 10 new Member States opted to embrace the intergovernmental approach, a development that has had far-reaching consequences. For whereas until recently the federalist camp was still in the majority, enabling progress to be made in various domains of European integration, today Europe is slowly being paralysed by the standoff, as lately evidenced by the fate the has befallen the European Constitution. Apparently, in the 25-Member-State European Union it is even more difficult to reach a consensus about the key foundations and aims of European integration and the most important instruments required to attain those objectives. It would seem that the gap between the federalists and the intergovernmentalists has become unbridgeable. Some compromises may yet be found, but they no longer lead to unequivocal solutions and therefore tend to be received with resentment (rather than admiration) by the public, and thereby fuel general discontent. For example, some of the 'no' voters in the French referendum on the European Constitution maintained that the text clearly did not go far enough, whereas others strongly disagreed, maintaining it already went way too far.

All in all, a decisive choice now has to be taken. Should we opt for a mere free trade area or for a genuine political Europe? And should we opt for a merely intergovernmental approach or for a Community approach?

Of course, history points us very clearly in one direction, implying that the future of Europe lies in developing a political Europe resting on Community-based or federal foundations. It is an explosive concept, but the trend is unmistakeable, even if there have been some hiccups along the way. We have created a single market, have abolished internal borders, and have both a European Central Bank and our own European currency. Since the Treaty of Amsterdam we have been working on a Common Foreign Policy with a High

Representative. Schengen and Europol are realities. In short, it is clear that the European Union is inevitably developing into a political institution that respects the autonomy and powers of its Member States on the basis of a Constitution, but is also developing its own autonomous, European sphere of action in those domains where it has been authorised to do so. So the momentum to develop this political Europe needs to be generated afresh, not curbed.

THE EXPERIENCE OF THE UNITED STATES OF AMERICA

Whereas the process of European unification is unique, a similar debate and discussion took place in the late 18th century in North America when the constituent states of the United States joined together to form a federal state to which they ceded significant powers. In addition, federal America gradually expanded from the Atlantic to the Pacific Ocean. The parallel is striking: not only are the Member States assigning more and more powers to the European Union, but the Union is expanding from the Atlantic Ocean towards the Urals.

The American Federal Constitution dates from 1787 and was framed at the Constitutional Convention in Philadelphia. It is the oldest federal constitution in the world still in force and has hardly been amended since 1789. However, the birth of the Constitution was not easy.

Right after 1776, at the outbreak of the American Revolution, the 13 new independent states that had formerly been British colonies formalised their cooperative arrangement. Adopting the Articles of Confederation, they created a union that they had already established informally in their struggle for independence. Those Articles created the 'United States of America'. It did not have a government, but it did have a Continental Congress in which each of the 13 states had one vote. The union was weak. The Articles allowed states to leave the confederation if they felt that their freedom and sovereignty were threatened. Moreover, Articles could only be amended by unanimous agreement between all members.

During the early years of the Articles, various attempts were made to give the union more power, since discord had arisen between the states on how to regulate and tax foreign trade. However, all these attempts failed due to a lack of consensus. A few important amendments were defeated by the opposition of a single state. This stalemate led to annoyance among the first group of Americans who would later become better known as the 'Federalists', led by James Madison, and in the end, the Federalists managed to convince Congress to call a Convention for the purpose of improving the Articles.

Once the Philadelphia Convention of 1787 had been called, it soon became clear that the Federalists wanted to go much further. They drew up a completely new Constitution under which the union had much greater powers. The Philadelphia Constitution had just seven articles. However, one article was particularly important where the process was concerned. Article VII stipulated, in contrast to the unanimity required under the Articles of Confederation, that approval by nine of the 13 states was enough to approve the Constitution and bring it into force.

All this greatly displeased the other side, known as the 'Anti-Federalists', who opposed the Constitution for many reasons, the main ones being fear of the power wielded by a strong, central government (their argument being that, after the British, they did not need another tyrant), the absence of a Bill of Rights (which was subsequently corrected during the ratification process) and, of course, the loss of power by the states themselves.

The discussions on the drafting of the Philadelphia Constitution focused on fundamental issues. Would the state be best governed by a representative democracy or by a direct democracy? Should the representatives in Congress be elected in proportion to the population, or should they be representatives of their state? What powers should the president have? He should not have too much power, to avoid the risk of authoritarian leadership, but at the same time he should have sufficient powers to help move things forward. Then again, should there be a division of powers, or would a mixed government be better? Could federal institutions declare state decrees to be invalid or should that not be possible?

All these questions prompted major disputes in newspapers and in the various states. Ultimately, in Philadelphia they opted clearly for a federal system. The new Constitution provided for the following division of powers:

- a federal executive branch led by a president;
- a federal legislative branch consisting of a Congress with two chambers: a House of Representatives, whose members are elected on a proportional basis and, a Senate with a given number of representatives from each state;
- a judicial branch, with a federal court created to protect individuals and states from excessive federal interference.

Now the task was to convince America's citizens about the Constitution, which was not so easy given the influence wielded by the Anti-Federalists. However, the most important argument was the widespread realisation that in the War of Independence the 13 former colonies had only managed to win because they fought under a united command. Had they been left to their own devices, the 13 colonies would have lost the war. So it was no wonder that the commander-in-chief of the War of Independence, George Washington, was not only appointed chairman of the Philadelphia Convention, but went on to be elected the first 'federal' president.

But perhaps even more important for the success of the entire process was the stipulation that the Constitution would take effect upon ratification by nine of the 13 states. Five pro-federal states ratified it quickly. Massachusetts only voted 'yes' after the Federalists agreed to a national compromise, namely that a Bill of Rights would be added to the Constitution, enumerating the rights and freedoms that the federal government also had to respect. Massachusetts was followed by another three states, making a total of nine. For the remaining four states, there was a clear choice between going along or being left out. Virginia – the home state of Madison and Washington, but also a state where the Anti-Federalists were very strong – realised that it would be politically, geographically and economically untenable to remain outside the union if the neighbouring states were part of it. But the ballot was still touch and go, resulting in a vote of 89 to 79. New York followed, with a vote of 30 to 27. Ultimately, the only state that voted against, Rhode Island – which had something of a reputation as a rogue state – had no choice but to organise a second vote, joining the union in 1790.

However, this did not mean that the Anti-Federalists and the Articles of Confederation vanished overnight. For nearly a century, from 1776 to 1861, the United States was – in many respects and despite the 1787 Constitution – governed as a confederation, in which the states had far greater powers than the federal government. The federal government was especially weak during that period. In fact, it had hardly any departments (ministries) and the president had no staff. The biggest federal department in the 19th century was in fact the postal service.

Similarly, it was a century and a half before the United States created a standing army worthy of the name. Until 1861, the American federal army never had more than 15,000 soldiers, even though the country already had a population of 32 million. When the prestigious Military Academy at West Point was founded in 1802, the president had a total of 3,350 armed soldiers at his disposal. In times of war, the US twice raised an enormous army 'from nothing' (3 million soldiers in 1864, 4 million in 1918), but on both occasions it disbanded the army after the war. Not until 1941, when the country had to mobilise for a third time, did the US maintain a large army, a century and a half after its independence.

For federal America, the turning point was the Civil War (1861-1865). The Civil War was a late offshoot of the Articles of Confederation of 1777, because the southern states in particular had never really been enamoured of the Federal Constitution. It was on the basis of the Articles of Confederation that 11 of the then 30 states seceded from the Union in 1861 to establish the Confederated States of America. Only after the Civil War did a federal government gradually develop. The opening up of the Far West, the development of railways and the advent of heavy industry (the individual states were too small for the business world) played just as critical role in the government's development as the Constitution.

However, in 1929, the year of the massive global economic crash, just 1% of America's GDP went to the federal government. Incidentally, this is comparable to the financial resources of the European Union in 2005. Twenty-four years later, in 1953, the figure had risen to 17%, levelling off later at around 20%. The stock market crash led to a big leap forward for America's federal government. Not until those years, did the United States – under the impetus of President Franklin D. Roosevelt's New Deal – forge a fully fledged federal government. The poor economy and the high unemployment rate meant that the United States was once again faced with a decision: either to continue fading away or to pursue a genuine federal economic policy. Apart from the social model that the federation developed, it is still obvious today that the decision to go with the federal model was correct. And this provides a clear hint as to what Europe has to do.

A NEW EUROPE

Just as the call for cooperation in the United States grew louder after two wars, the War of Independence and the American Civil War, European unification was prompted by the traumatic experiences of two World Wars. When, 50 years on, we compare the Union's objectives of securing peace, stability and prosperity with what has been attained, we cannot help but reach the conclusion that the European Union has done what it set out to attain.

Those citizens born in a free Western Europe after 1945 are the first since many centuries not to have experienced a war or dictatorship. And as the Union has expanded, the area of stability in Europe has grown along with it, first taking in Greece, Spain and Portugal, then the countries of Central and Eastern Europe, which barely 15 years ago were still gripped by Communism.

At the same time, European integration has prompted some giddy economic growth. When Ireland acceded to the Union in 1973, it was the poorest country in the whole of Western Europe. Now it is one of the five richest countries in the world. The Spanish economic miracle is another example. European integration has indisputably proved to be a magic formula for eliminating differences on the continent of Europe closing gaps in prosperity. As such,

European integration has undoubtedly been the most important social project of the past 50 years.

But that doesn't mean the battle has been fought. Today's crisis with regard to the European Constitution conceals a very serious danger that a number of major Member States will regard the issue as having been settled and form a '*directoire*', as the French Interior Minister Nicolas Sarkozy recently suggested. The euro zone is also under threat. A few months ago one member go the Italian government argued in favour of the reintroduction of the lira, an indication that it is at least conceivable that the euro will come under pressure if we do not swiftly manage to develop a successful socio-economic strategy in Europe.

In a nutshell, the European Union is like a bicycle. It must keep rolling forwards or it will topple over. The consequences would be disastrous. No more free movement of persons; instead, back with customs posts and identity checks. No more free movement of goods; instead, the re-establishment of customs posts and import duty on most products. No common euro either, but the need for anyone travelling through Europe to keep 10 different currencies in their wallet. All of a sudden, the peace and prosperity we have built up over the past 50 years would all be a fair bit less self-evident.

Those European citizens alive today who *did* live through the war and experience poverty understand this, and they are also the strongest advocates of any European progress. Younger Europeans, on the other hand, who never had to endure such horrors, hold the view that Europe has to mean more today. Europe must not merely provide a response to the problems of 60 years ago, but also come up with answers to present and future problems. In other words, we must launch a revamped European project that effectively taps into the longings of younger European citizens in particular. Furthermore, we must give the Union the instruments it needs to enable it to respond to its citizens' many fears and doubts.

The United States of America only managed to overcome the Great Depression after the stock market crash of 1929 by putting together a federal socio-economic policy. Likewise, only by embracing a fresh approach and with new powers can Europe overcome the depression of today. The same applies to cross-border organised crime or the need for Europe to take its place in the international political arena. A new approach is also needed in these areas, so that Europe can speak with one voice and act in unison.

Opting for a new Europe will entail fresh powers, a new system for financing the Union, and the establishment of new institutions. At the same time it will also mean the European Union putting an end to all the quibbling and politicking practised far too often today. If 'Brussels' is regarded merely as a bureaucratic machine that mainly concerns itself with promulgating countless Kafkaesque measures, then it primarily has itself to blame. Take the proposal about imposing opening and closing hours on shops throughout the entire Union. Every Member State has different opinions on this, sometimes owing to historical and cultural differences, but in other cases even because of climatic factors. People in Athens have no interest in going shopping in the searing midday heat, so shops there shut at lunch time, but remain open until late in the evening. In Helsinki the situation is quite different. So it is folly to seek to impose European rules in this connection.

Certainly, the Union interferes too much in some domains. The principle of subsidiarity – a difficult concept that boils down to saying that the Union may only deal with issues where cross-border cooperation entails a genuine benefit – has in actual fact remained a dead letter. The European Union has no role to play in areas of policy such as culture or sport; likewise it should steer clear of areas like the organisation of health care, social security, education, and the manner in which the civil service or judicial apparatus is run. This is a selection of the matters that have to be left entirely up to the Member States. And citizens don't expect any European initiatives in these areas since Europe has no added value to offer here: on the contrary.

This latter observation must constitute our starting point today. New powers for the new Europe must gradually deliver some added benefit. They must be core tasks that make Europe more powerful, but at the same time less patronising. There are essentially five such tasks.

FIVE TASKS FOR THE NEW EUROPE

(1) European social and economic governance and strategy

For years now, Europe has suffered from slack economic growth and unacceptably high unemployment. Amongst other things, Europe's continuing negative performance has exerted pressure on the European Social Model, prompting some to challenge the very model itself. But that is not where the cause of Europe's problems lies. We cannot turn things around by drastically slashing social protection in the Union – just the opposite, in fact.

One of the main reasons for Europe's poor performance is that in recent years the euro – the most tangible and radical achievement of European integration – has not been supported by a common economic and social policy. The Union's economic policy is limited to certain directives and to the requirements set out in the Stability and Growth Pact, but these only apply in the euro zone. Social policy consists mainly of employment guidelines and provisions governing safety in the workplace. And the sole role of the European Central Bank is to fight inflation, with scarcely any support for a broader European approach to social and economic issues. Although it was launched five years ago, the Lisbon strategy has not led to any progress either. We have not moved beyond formulating praiseworthy goals, such as Europe's ambition to become the most competitive knowledge-based economy in the world by 2010. And yet that goal seems further away than ever. The method developed for this purpose – the 'open coordination method' – is far too casual. Simply drawing up tables and reports comparing the receipts and results of the Member States with each other does not really bring much pressure to bear.

However, nobody can deny that a common approach pays off. It was that kind of approach that allowed us to eliminate most of the customs borders for goods and capital and to control successfully monetary disorder. The Stability Pact signed in 1997 has since become essential for the health and success of monetary union and the euro, which was introduced on 1 January 2002. In the space of just a few years, it has prompted the euro zone countries to pursue a sound budgetary policy. After all, balanced budgets and falling government debt are key conditions for growth and employment. They create consumer confidence and they lead to lower interest rates and higher investments. But it must be acknowledged that there has been less and less impetus from the Pact in recent years due to the lack of a comprehensive economic strategy. On top of that, budgetary discipline in many Member States has gradually slackened off due to the absence of hoped-for economic growth, both within the Union and within the euro zone.

Nevertheless, the euro is a perfect example of why we must pursue a common social and economic policy. Only by taking a common approach can we once again make the European economy a world-class competitor. Competitiveness is an absolute precondition for boosting employment in Europe and maintaining the European Social Model.

When it comes to economic growth and the creation of new jobs, Europe has trailed behind the United States, India, Japan and especially China for some time now, and it is expected that the gap between Europe and those growth areas will continue to widen. There are many reasons for this development, one being the relentless globalisation of the world economy.

New players are arriving every day. New markets are opening up. Hordes of new consumers are coming forward. All of this might just rush right past the European economy if it does not adopt a comprehensive, common strategy to free itself of its internal shortcomings and structural weaknesses.

The first such weakness is the unilateral financing of the European Social Model. Social protection in Europe is almost exclusively financed by taxes levied on labour, a situation that undermines the productive power of society and could well result in the loss of Europe's industrial infrastructure. The second weakness of the European economy is the heavy administrative burden in many EU Member States. Lastly, the European single market is not yet complete and it is making progress far too slowly.

The Member States' responses to these structural shortcomings are still far too disparate, especially in the wake of enlargement. Most Member States are trying to implement reforms, some successfully, others less so. On the other hand, most of the new Member States are trying to derive maximum benefit from their competitive edge, which is derived from their level of social protection and corresponding low taxes. Accordingly, Europe is seeing the slow development of a 'niche economy' of low wages, low taxes and limited social protection, which is likely to lead to outright dumping between the Member States, a development that not only impacts on the European Social Model but also directly undermines the cohesion of the single market. So no wonder the citizens of Europe have fears and doubts about these developments and wonder where Europe's political leadership is.

That political leadership must come from a European social and economic 'cabinet' tasked with developing a coherent economic strategy for the European Union. In other words, a social and economic cabinet should be set up within the European Commission and run solely by those commissioners who are responsible for matters linked to that strategy. That cabinet must then develop a forward-looking social and economic strategy which can be submitted as quickly as possible to the European Council and the Eurogroup.

The strategy must primarily be based on and lead to a convergence code in the Union. Convergence was the method successfully used in the Stability Pact during the creation of the monetary Union. Unlike harmonisation, convergence means defining 'fluctuation bands' within which the economies of the EU Member States must develop, so that they can work together on achieving a more integrated and more competitive European economy. The maximum limits of the bands are the values that must not be exceeded in order to avoid undermining the strength of the economy. The minimum limits are the values that must be achieved at the very least to guarantee the foundations for social protection and sustainable development. The minimum and maximum values pertain to the most important components that are crucial to the social and economic climate, such as the flexibility or rigidity of the labour market, the duration of working life, the level of protection given to workers, the magnitude of public levies, tax pressure on companies and other factors. The use of bands instead of fixed standards or vague objectives makes it possible – much more effectively than in the past – to take account of the specific features of each national economy. For instance, one Member State will be geared more towards industry, whilst another will focus more on services. One Member State will have different traditions regarding social protection than another Member State. On the other hand, the bands must be relevant, meaning that the gap between its outer limits must not be too extreme. The gap must be defined in such a way that it prompts a number of Member States to conform to it, minimum levels so that they can take part in the accomplishments of the European Social Model, and maximum levels so that they can make a genuine contribution to a more integrated and, at the same time, more 'battle-ready' European economy.

The second component in the new strategy is a thorough reform of the tax systems in Europe, the sole aim being to boost the power of the European economy compared to the rest of the world. The European economy is a very open economy. The high taxes we impose on workers, employees, the self-employed and businesses have created a situation where we are now exporting our jobs instead of our products. Our companies are moving out and creating jobs on other continents. The result is less income to finance social protection. The only path we can take entails thoroughly changing how we finance the system, more specifically making a radical shift from direct taxes and social security contributions to indirect taxes or other levies. After all, indirect taxes, for instance, are neutral and do not exert any direct pressure on production costs. They do not impact on exports. Thanks to the indexing mechanisms found in various parts of Europe, they also help to guarantee social benefits and the ongoing purchasing power of the lowest-wage earners. Indirect taxes make no distinction as to the origin of the product; they are levied on imported products and services, as well as on products and services produced within the Union. They are paid by working and non-working individuals. And, above all, they keep social Europe on its feet.

A recent European Commission study explored the potential positive impact of this kind of approach. Shifting just one percent of GDP from direct to indirect taxes would yield a 0.4% increase in our economic prosperity over five years. After five years, employment would rise by half of one percent. If the shift is not factored into an indexing mechanism, the growth forecasts are slightly higher. However, the results would only become really spectacular if the countries in Europe derived 40% (compared to 33% today) of their income from indirect taxes. For Germany and Belgium, for instance, this would yield – in the best-case scenario – a 3.8% increase in employment, translating into 160,000 new jobs for Belgium alone. Over 10 years, the economies of both countries would grow by more than 3%. If, instead of 40%, we were to take half from indirect taxes, then Europe's economic growth over five years would be nearly 4% higher! This is the kind of performance that Europe can only dream about today.

Another component in the new economic strategy for Europe is the development of a new wave of European technology.

(2) A new wave of European technology

Throughout history, only those cultures that have sought out the limits of the possible and, even more importantly, the impossible, have made progress. Major inventions have always emerged in countries that were world leaders or on their way to the top. It is no coincidence that the countries that were home to such inventions were always those that exerted a strong pull on painters, writers, philosophers and scientists. After all, creative minds attract more creativity and innovation. As the Americans say: "success breeds success".

It would be wrong to maintain that there is a lack of creativity in Europe today. European technological innovation can hold its own with the United States and Japan. Just look at such enormous and successful projects as Airbus in the aviation sector, Ariane in space travel, and the high-speed train. Yet Europe earmarks too little money for research and development. In terms of financial efforts for innovation and patent registrations, the European Union lags far behind the United States and especially Japan. The lack of a single European patent is a serious obstacle for European businesses and research centres. The European patent was one of the key objectives of the Lisbon Strategy, but five years on we are still arguing about what language should be used to draft European patents.

Delays like this pose a threat to the future of Europe. When it comes to labour costs, Europe will never really be able to compete with the low-wage countries. Nor can we compete in terms of raw materials. In addition, we are almost totally dependent on other continents for our energy requirements. This means that we Europeans have to focus on innovation. That is why one of the core tasks of a new Europe must be to invest in forward-looking initiatives. Europe must invest more in scientific and technological research. In addition to conventional areas, like space travel and medicine, where we in Europe do excellent work, our main efforts focus on everything to do with the environment and ICT (information and communication technology).

The environment is one of the leading policy areas where cross-border cooperation at European level is urgently needed. By now it is clear that we will not easily achieve the Kyoto targets on emissions of harmful substances. Placing restrictions on companies not only makes our economy less competitive, for the umpteenth time, but will not be sufficient to enable us to attain the set objectives. The solution to this dilemma lies in more innovation. If a Japanese carmaker manages to achieve a breakthrough in hybrid car engines, then Europe must be able to make breakthroughs in other areas. In that sense, it is good to see that the first experimental nuclear fusion reactor is to be built in Europe. Moreover, innovation in the energy sector is not only important for the environment, but can also reduce our dependence on other continents and our vulnerability to price fluctuations. We simply must not make the typical mistake of allowing the resources earmarked for innovation to be frittered away. On the contrary, we must pool our resources at European level so that we can allocate them strategically for innovation.

In terms of ICT, the role that Europe can play is somewhat less obvious. After all, historically speaking, businesses take the lead in rapid developments. Government generally has a hard time keeping up. Moreover, some countries in the European Union are already world leaders, whereas others are just taking their first steps. Yet Europe has seen just how important a role ICT plays in economic and cultural progress. The role of the European government is to create a secure, forward-looking regulatory framework for rapid technological evolution. In this connection, the liberalisation of the information and communication sectors must be a priority. In the battle with their American and Asian rivals, European companies can only survive if they can face up to the competition unfettered and unhindered by excessive regulation.

We must be so bold as to go further in a new Europe. After all, the impact of ICT extends beyond the sector itself. ICT is the driving force behind a true economic and social revolution. As the government, we have a duty to ensure that nobody is left behind in this revolution. That is why it is important for Europe to have world-class information superhighways and communications infrastructure. That is the foundation for a forward-looking economy and also a tool for further integration. Like Jacques Delors' Trans-European Networks (TENs) of the 1980s, where the plan was to interconnect the motorway networks of the Member States, today Europe needs to develop a network of information superhighways (IHEN).

To achieve all this, the new Europe must substantially increase its research and development budget. In concrete terms, this means we must set aside half our expenditure on competitiveness for R&D, whilst a quarter of the expenditure in regions of the Member States that enjoy access to structural funds must be assigned to R&D projects. All in all, this will entail increasing the share of expenditure on R&D to make it the second largest budget item after expenditure on agriculture.

(3) The European area of justice and security

In addition to worrying about the wilting economy and slack employment, the citizens of Europe are deeply concerned about crime in Europe. Crimes such as ram-raiding, car-jacking and burglary are increasingly being committed by roving gangs of wrongdoers. For the last 10 years or so, some organised crime has been controlled by gangs from Eastern Europe. There is no doubt that the national police forces of various countries are doing a good job tackling these criminal activities, and a lot of networks have been smashed, but since these gangs operate across borders, the only effective way to counter them is to have a strong European cross-border approach.

In addition to crime, we must not forget that since the tragic events of 11 September 2001 in the United States, Europe has also suffered from the scourge of international terrorism. The barbaric attacks in Istanbul, Madrid and London deeply shocked us all and taught us that we must always be vigilant. Clearly, national anti-terrorism units will not be able stop dangers of this magnitude alone. Indeed, it was this realisation that recently led to the appointment of a special terrorism coordinator in Europe. However, unless the representative is given appropriate powers, the appointment will just be a waste of time. Justice and security must be the third core task of the new Europe.

The European arrest warrant, under which criminals sought in one country can be arrested in another and immediately extradited to the country were the crimes took place, is a step in the right direction. But this alone will not make the problem go away. People are rightly demanding a more thorough approach. That is why we must create a 'European area for justice and security' as quickly as possible. Within the European Union, we must also have a systematic exchange of data between police services, magistrates and security services. This is how it will become impossible for someone like Fourniret to go about his business undisturbed for years. Europol must be expanded into a European investigation office and Eurojust into a European prosecutor's office. Likewise, the trade in human beings and illegal immigration can only be efficiently countered at European level. To prevent rejected asylum-seekers from taking advantage of previous agreements and trying their luck in another country, it would be good to establish a European immigration policy and a single European immigration service.

In developing the European area for justice and security, the last thing we want to do is create a new European bureaucracy. It makes no sense to create a special European body in addition to the specialist services of the Member States. That would just lead to even more red tape and maybe create an even bigger gap between policy and reality. Instead, we should opt to join forces. For instance, a European immigration service should not bring with it an army of new officials or take on new duties. What we need to do is bring together people from the existing national bodies within the new body. These people will coordinate policy and make it more efficient. The administrative burden has to be reduced and policy harmonised.

(4) European diplomacy

The war in the Balkans and the war in Iraq showed us once and for all that Europe can only make its voice heard on the world stage when it takes unanimous and vigorous action. There must never be a repeat of the scenario where a powerless Europe has to call the White House to put an end to an armed conflict on its own continent, as was the case during the Balkan wars. And there must be no repeat of the situation where Europe is so divided that a mere discussion between the heads of state and government is impossible, as was the case with Iraq. Iraq was only placed on the European agenda when the dice had already been cast, positions had already been taken and European impotence and division had become patently obvious.

If Europe – alongside the United States, Russia, China, Japan and other up-and-coming regional powers – wants to have a voice in the global forum and intends to speak with one voice within that forum, then it must work on developing a genuine European foreign policy. Even the large EU Member States, with populations of 60 or 80 million, are small compared with the real superpowers. Where Iraq is concerned, the United States did not have to take account of Europe because Europe was divided and incapable of taking a stance. Even the most loyal American ally within the European Union had scarcely any influence in Washington.

A true European foreign policy necessitates a single foreign minister who represents Europe and is able to speak, on equal terms, with the foreign ministers of the United States, Russia and China. He or she must be empowered to take action and get things moving, not just to look at situations. In addition to foreign and trade policy, we also need to devise a common development policy. The developing countries in particular would welcome this. In the past, the various European countries have often ended up working against each other rather than with each other. Accordingly, there is a real need for greater consistency and coherence between the policies of the various Member States and the Union. With Europe, we should pool 0.7% of our resources and earmark them for targeted uses. In so doing, we can use 'development cooperation' with many countries currently facing difficulties to evolve towards 'cooperation development'.

If we want to develop a common foreign policy, then we also need to create a single diplomatic service for Europe. Today, every country in the Union, large and small alike, has an embassy, an ambassador and one or more diplomats almost everywhere in the world. If the various diplomatic services were merged into a single European diplomatic corps, the flow of information would be improved. This approach would also save money. Lastly, a common foreign policy with a single foreign minister and a single diplomatic service could entail us opting for Europe to have a seat on the UN Security Council. This could only add greater weight to our voice. It would also encourage the other continents to achieve greater cooperation, establish larger political entities and in so doing create more global peace, stability and prosperity.

(5) The European army

Fifty years after the collapse of the European Defence Community, plans to pursue a European defence mechanism are one of our key interests. The impetus for this came from the French-British summit in Saint-Malo in 1997 and, to a greater extent, from the common proposals of Germany, France, Luxembourg and Belgium in 2003. In the meantime, a European Defence Agency and a Strategic Analysis and Planning Unit have been created. This unit was needed to enable the preparation of autonomous operations by the European Union.

However, this is not enough. European foreign policy will only be credible if there is a true European defence, in other words a European army. Here, we should call a spade a spade. That was often a problem in the past. The fate of the European headquarters is an example of this. The proposal was drafted by Germany, France, Luxembourg and Belgium in 2003, but ran into stiff resistance from a small number of Member States. Finally, nine months later, agreement was reached on a 'civilian military unit'. This unit will handle planning and management for autonomous European operations, but cannot be referred to as 'headquarters' and must not be located in a separate building. The point of this is to maintain the illusion that the European Union is not actually going about developing its own military capability. This kind of Potemkin-like manoeuvring must be stopped.

The European Union must have its own military arm, comprising forces made available by the Member States. The Member States must earmark a minimum percentage of their GDP for defence spending – the aim being to ensure the credibility of Europe's defence. Naturally, there will still be national armed forces, which can serve as a pool from which to draw when putting together the European defence force and can be used to fulfil other duties too. In principle, only the European defence force can operate outside the territory of the European Union. It can be deployed for evacuation, peacemaking and peacekeeping operations, or in specific cases even preventively.

Of course, this European defence capability is not a strategic move against the United States, nor is it meant to undermine the Atlantic Alliance – on the contrary. A common European defence means that Europe is a fully fledged, battle-ready partner of the United States. A common European defence will supplement the Alliance with a strong, credible European pillar. A European defence will create the balance we need within NATO. It must enable us to improve the coordination of our common fight against terror. It is important that Europe and the United States work on a common strategy – a strategy devised by full partners.

NEW FINANCING FOR A NEW EUROPE

The recent discussion about the new financial perspectives made it clear once again that European heads of state and government are finding it increasingly difficult to agree on the European Union's financial framework. Once again, this is an example of a fundamental difference of opinion that is threatening to paralyse the European Union, because the statistics by themselves effectively conceal clashing visions of European integration. Some Member States want to keep the European Union's budget as small as possible. They want to cut spending on regional solidarity between poor and rich regions, on research and development, on cooperation on justice and security and on European foreign and defence policy. On the other hand, other Member States want to give the European Union sufficient resources to carry out its many tasks.

On top of that, the entire debate is being poisoned by the contrast between 'net payers' and 'net recipients' and by the argument for a 'fair return' which, as a result of the introduction of the UK's rebate in 1984, crept into the debate on the European budget.

The debate between net payers and net recipients is likely to get bogged down in a situation where, in every instance, we have to calculate down to the last cent, to make sure that this or that Member State does not pay or receive too much. In the long term, this is deadly for Europe, which is why we must switch to a financing system that is based on our own resources. The European Union must be able to rely on full budgetary autonomy. To this end, the national payments calculated on the basis of gross national income must be cut back. It would be better to derive the Union's income from taxes levied on consumption or eco-taxes. We should follow the practice used in the United States, i.e. anyone buying something in a shop should be able to look at their receipt and see what percentage of the cost is going to finance Europe and what percentage will disappear into national coffers. The big advantage of this approach is that it is totally transparent to citizens. This practice would also make it much clearer just how small the European Union's budget is in comparison with the budgets of its Member States. Moreover it will blow the myth that Europe is awash with cash.

Even though financing for the Union needs to change, solidarity must remain. Solidarity between richer and poorer Member States and the regions is one of the cornerstones of European integration. Over the last 50 years, European integration has proven to be the most effective way for eliminating differences in development levels within Europe. This must remain possible in the future, too. And it is not just the poorer Member States that are better off because of it.

So, solidarity is essential. But care must be taken to ensure that broad social support for solidarity remains. Large imbalances are not good. That is why it is a good idea to cap contributions from the individual Member States. Otherwise, there is a danger that the citizens of the wealthier Member States will end up losing their readiness to bear the financial burden. It makes no sense for Germany to contribute one quarter of the entire European budget. Nor does it make sense for Member States at a comparable level of economic development not to contribute proportionally to the European budget. These kinds of distortions will become untenable in the long run and simply encourage the debate on a 'fair return'. For instance, we could make it a rule that the contributions from richer Member States could never exceed a specified ceiling, expressed as a still-to-be-decided percentage of the European average.

NEW INSTITUTIONS FOR A NEW EUROPE

Powerful European policies are impossible without efficient, transparent and democratic institutions. Political institutions acquire greater democratic legitimacy when it is clear what their tasks and powers are. The institutions must also be recognisable. That is why it is best for them to have a face.

We definitely need to get away from incomprehensible Eurospeak, in which long and difficult descriptions are used to gloss over or bypass bold decisions. This kind of jargon is the fastest way to make the gap between the citizens' European dream and reality unbridgeable. So we should stop talking about the president-in-office of the European Council when what we mean is the president of Europe. Why is Javier Solana called the High Representative for the Common Foreign and Security Policy when he is actually the European minister for foreign affairs? An even more striking example of bureaucratic language is giving the executive branch of Europe the ridiculous name 'Commission', while in the rest of the world it is called 'the government'.

So, if we want to once again make sure that Europe is an attractive project, a project in which younger generations can believe, we will have to create recognisable institutions with understandable names and clearly defined tasks.

We must also ensure that each of the three democratic branches of government actually has the expected powers and duties. Only in this way can we respond to the general question as to whether Europe is the right level at which to tackle the challenges facing us today.

First and foremost, we must have a genuine European government, which, just like in all parliamentary democracies, has executive powers. The European government, which must have the confidence of Parliament, should be led by a president, who, in anticipation of direct, democratic elections by all European citizens, is appointed by the European Parliament and the Council. Direct elections will ensure that the European debate is pursued by citizens. Today, this only happens if there is a referendum – and then people immediately complain that their views on Europe are not given sufficient consideration.

The legislative branch must, of course, be the preserve of the European Parliament, which, as in most federal state structures, is bicameral. On the one hand, we have the European Parliament, which is comprised proportionally of representatives of the population of the Member States; on the other, we have the Council, which consists of representatives of the governments of the Member States. This arrangement offers an ideal way to strike a balance between the general European interest and the specific interests of individual Member States.

A 'UNITED STATES OF EUROPE' IN AN 'ORGANISATION OF EUROPEAN STATES'

Europe has reached a crossroads. At this juncture, we do not need institutional tinkering or a spot of Community DIY to turn the tide. We must guard against taking the easy way out. Either we let Europe atrophy until it is nothing more than a free trade zone, or we commit to the dream of Europe's citizenry and opt for a political Europe, a new Europe.

In France and the Netherlands too, a majority of people want more Europe, not less. The Constitution was not rejected because it was too ambitious, but because it was not ambitious enough. What we need is a clear project, a clearly defined objective and the political will to achieve that. We need a new blueprint with which, rather than slipping into a patronising mode, Europe focuses on its core tasks, a Europe that recognises the identity and cultural singularity of the Member States, a Europe that has powerful institutions and budgetary autonomy.

Ideally, this qualitative leap forward would be taken by all 25 Member States. But recent experiences in the European Council, experiences in negotiating the Treaty of Nice, the Laeken Declaration, the Constitution and the financial framework give us reason to fear that this may no longer be possible. The Member States of the European Union no longer constitute a homogeneous group that wants to move in the same direction with Europe. In some Member States, the political aim of the European project is negated. Some view the European Union as nothing more than an economic cooperation agreement or, even worse, a gravy train.

Consequently, it is likely that only a smaller group of Member States will be prepared to take this step. In that case, it makes little sense to wait until everyone wishes to come along, for that would merely be waiting for a train that will never come. This being the case, a core group within the European Union must seize the initiative.

In the best-case scenario, this group will consist of the countries belonging to the euro zone or which at least plan to join it shortly. Opting to join the euro zone has various advantages. One obvious benefit is that it offers consolidated, established cooperation. Moreover, this cooperation has already shown that it is capable of delivering, because we have the euro. Our children have already forgotten francs and lira. In addition, the euro zone is not 'à la carte Europe', for the criteria for acceding to it are clear. Budget deficits, national debts and inflation all have to be kept in check. Finally, the euro zone comprises a number of Member States that have already embraced a common destiny.

These Member States, and those that accede within the near future, must now display the ambition to develop a common social and economic policy in support of the euro. They must join forces to fight slack economic growth, unemployment and also tackle major societal problems like fighting crime. They need to develop common legislation on minimum social standards and taxation. In addition, they must join forces to boost R&D and develop trans-European information networks. Lastly, they must take the lead in establishing a common army and speaking with a single voice on foreign policy issues.

The existence of opposing views means it is not inconceivable that we will see the emergence of two concentric circles in Europe, namely a political core, a 'United States of Europe' comprising the euro zone, surrounded by a confederation of states, an 'Organisation of European States'. Of course, the political core is not opposed to broader cooperation in Europe. Every Member State will continue to be a full part of the broader integration process. The ultimate aim is for all Member States to join the new Europe.

For this reason, the new Europe must not be exclusive under any circumstances. All those Member States that wish to join should be allowed to do so, be they old or new. The sole precondition is that they must wish to take part unconditionally in the overall political project. In addition, the creation of a political union makes it possible to continue enlarging the Union without any major problems. After all, enlargement is needed to expand the area of peace, stability and prosperity across the entire European continent. This approach also constitutes the ideal solution to a problem that is becoming ever more acutely felt: the absence of an interim stage between when a country knocks on Europe's door and when it actually becomes a member of the Union. Provided that applicant Member States met the required criteria, they could always accede to the Union without having to join immediately the demanding core group.

A EUROPEAN REFERENDUM

The purpose of this manifesto is to trace out the main lines of a European project capable of attracting younger generations. Once all or many of the Member States are committed to building up a new Europe, the project must obviously be capable of withstanding a test by the citizens of Europe. That is why a referendum must be organised to put the question to all the citizens of those Member States taking part, a referendum to be organised on a European referendum day – i.e. on the same day and at the same time everywhere – as is current practice for European elections.

Many millions of Europeans want a Europe that offers a powerful and inspiring answer to the challenges with which we are confronted today and will face tomorrow. They do not want some half-hearted or bureaucratic answer. They want us to make clear choices and take clear decisions. They want to be given a plan they can believe in. If we meet the citizens' expectations, then an overwhelming majority of them will support and show their approval for the new Europe.